Knit Bright
Scarves, Hats, Booties, and More

KRISTIN SPURKLAND

Martingale®
Create with Confidence

Knit Bright: Scarves, Hats, Booties, and More
© 2013 by Kristin Spurkland

Martingale®
19021 120th Ave. NE, Ste. 102
Bothell, WA 98011-9511 USA
ShopMartingale.com

Printed in China

18 17 16 15 14 13   8 7 6 5 4 3 2 1

Library of Congress Cataloging-in-Publication Data is available upon request.

ISBN: 978-1-60468-313-4

Mission Statement
Dedicated to providing quality products
and service to inspire creativity.

Contents

Striped Hat

This snug-fitting hat looks great on people with short hair or bald heads, such as babies, men, or anyone undergoing chemotherapy.

Sizes

To fit: 6 mos–1 yr (2–4 yrs, Child–Adult)
Circumference: 16¼ (18½, 21)"

Materials

Yarn: Approx 120 yds *each* of 3 colors per hat of 100% wool DK-weight yarn (**3**); label yarns A and B for rib and C for crown

Needles: Size 6 circular needle (16" long) or size required to obtain gauge, size 6 double-pointed needles (dpns)

Notions: Stitch marker, tapestry needle

Gauge

22 sts and 30 rows = 4" in St st on size 6 needle

Rib Pattern

Rnd 1: With A, *K1, P1, rep from * around.
Rnd 2: Knit with B.
Rnd 3: With B, *K1, P1, rep from * around.
Rnd 4: Knit with A.

Hat

With A and circular needle, CO 98 (112, 126) sts. Join, pm at beg of rnd. Beg Rib patt, alternating colors as indicated and carrying color not in use up inside of hat. Twist yarns loosely when changing colors. Work rnds 1–4 a total of 4 (5, 6) times; then work rnd 1 once more. Change to C and knit 1 rnd. Break A and B. Purl 1 rnd, and then knit 1 rnd.

Shape Crown

Next rnd: Cont with C, *K12 (14, 16), K2tog, rep from * around.
Next rnd: Knit.
Rep last 2 rnds, working 1 less st before dec with each dec rnd and switching to dpns when necessary until you have completed K7 (9, 10), K2tog rnd. From this point on, omit plain knit rnd between dec rnds. Cont to dec every rnd until you have completed K2tog rnd—7 sts. Break yarn, thread through tapestry needle, and draw through rem sts.

Perfect for Chemo Caps

This snug and flattering hat works beautifully as a chemo cap. Make them in many different color combinations—perhaps a different hat for every day of the week—and be sure to make the hat out of a soft, warm, easy-to-care-for yarn.

Rolled-Edge Hat

You can knit this hat, with its classic stripes and rolled-edge finish, in an evening or two. It's a perfect "gift-in-a-hurry" project.

Sizes

To fit: Preemie (0–6 mos, 1 yr, 2 yrs, 3–4 yrs)*
Circumference: 14 (16½, 17¾, 19, 20¼)"

* To ensure proper fit, measure the child's head before choosing a size. If the measurement falls between sizes, consider making the larger size, so the child can grow into the hat rather than out of it.

Materials

Yarn: Approx 108 yds *each* of 3 colors per hat of 100% cotton DK-weight yarn (**3**); label yarns A, B, and C
Needles: Size 5 circular needle (16" long) or size required to obtain gauge, one set size 5 dpn. Preemie and 0–6 months: use size 5 double-pointed needles (dpns) *only.*
Notions: Stitch marker, tapestry needle

Gauge

22 sts and 30 rows = 4" in St st on size 5 needle

Twisted Knitting Pattern

Knit through the back look to keep edge from flaring.
Rnds 1 and 3: K1tbl around.
Rnds 2 and 4: *K1tbl, sl 1 pw, rep from * around. For sizes that have an odd-number CO, end K1tbl.

Hat

With A, CO 77 (91, 98, 105, 112) sts. Join, pm at beg of rnd. Knit 4 rnds. Change to B, knit 2 rnds, then work 4 rnds in Twisted Knitting patt. Change to C, knit 4 rnds. Cont knitting 4 rnds of each color in St st as established until 7 stripes (5 stripes for preemie size) are completed from CO edge.

Shape Crown

Work 1 rnd of next color in sequence, then beg crown shaping.
Next rnd: *K9 (11, 12, 13, 14), K2tog, rep from * around.
Next rnd: Knit.
Rep last 2 rnds, working 1 less st before dec with each dec rnd and changing to dpn when necessary until you have completed K4 (4, 6, 8, 10), K2tog rnd. From this point forward, omit plain knit rnd between dec rnds. Cont to dec every rnd until you have completed the K2tog rnd—7 sts rem. Break yarn, thread through tapestry needle, and draw through rem sts.

Need a Smaller Hat?
The preemie hat size given here may be too big for some premature babies. To knit a smaller hat, follow the pattern as written, but use fingering-weight yarn and smaller needles. The result? A tiny hat for a tiny person!

Holiday Stocking

Despite the color work, this generously sized stocking works up quickly. Why not knit one for every member of the family?

Size
Diameter: 17¼"
Length: 24"

Materials
Yarn: 100% wool DK-weight yarn ③ in the following amounts and colors:
A: 220 yds (red)
B: 220 yds (green)
C: 110 yds (natural)
Needles: Size 3 circular needle (16" long) or size required to obtain gauge, size 2 circular needle (16" long), size 3 double-pointed needles (dpns)
Notions: Stitch markers, stitch holder, tapestry needle

Gauge
24 sts and 32 rows = 4" in St st on size 3 needle

Stocking
With A and size 2 needle, CO 102 sts. Join, pm at beg of rnd. Knit 12 rnds. Purl 1 rnd. Change to size 3 circular needle and knit 2 rnds. Beg Checkerboard chart. Work through rnd 11 of chart. Beg Figure chart, inc 1 st on either side of marker on rnd 1—104 sts. Work through rnd 24 of chart. Beg Stripe chart. On rnd 3, beg leg shaping.

Shape Leg
Cont stripe sequence as est.
Rnd 1: Knit first st after marker, SSK, work to last 3 sts of rnd, K2tog, knit last st.
Rnds 2–4: Knit.
Work rnds 1–4 a total of 9 times—86 sts rem. Cont to work even in Stripe chart until you have completed 9 stripes with B. Knit 1 rnd with C.

Beg Heel
Sl first 21 sts pw. Place next 43 sts on holder. Rejoining A and C, work heel flap back and forth in Salt and Pepper patt over 43 sts as follows:
Row 1: Sl 1 pw, *K1 with A, K1 with C, rep from *, end K1 with A and C held tog.
Row 2: Sl 1 pw, *P1 with C, P1 with A, rep from *, end P1 with A and C held tog.
Work these 2 rows a total of 8 times. Work row 1 once more. Purl next row with A only—a total of 18 rows worked. Break C.

Turn Heel
With A, turn heel as follows:
Row 1: Sl 1 pw, K25, K2tog, K1, turn.
Row 2: Sl 1 pw, P9, P2tog, P1, turn.
Row 3: Sl 1 pw, K10, K2tog, K1, turn.
Row 4: Sl 1 pw, P11, P2tog, P1, turn.
Cont in this manner until all heel sts have been worked, ending with completed WS row. Break yarn.

Beg Gusset

Sl 14 sts pw, replace marker, rejoin A. K13, PU 10 sts along heel flap, pm (this will be a gusset marker), knit across 43 sts on holder, pm (another gusset marker), PU 10 sts along heel flap, K14 (these are same sts you slipped at beg of rnd)—90 sts. Knit 1 rnd.

Shape Gusset

As you shape gusset, cont to work stripe sequence as established on leg.

Next rnd: Knit to 2 sts before first gusset marker, K2tog, knit to next gusset marker, SSK, knit to end of rnd.

Next rnd: Knit.

Rep these 2 rnds a total of 9 times, changing to dpns when necessary—72 sts. Cont to work stripe patt until you have completed 16 stripes from top of leg with B. Knit 1 rnd C. Break B and C.

Shape Toe

With A, knit 1 rnd.

Next rnd: *K10, K2tog, rep from * around.

Next rnd: Knit.

Rep these 2 rnds, working 1 less st before dec with each dec rnd until you have completed K2, K2tog rnd. From this point forward, omit plain knit rnds between dec rnds. Cont to dec every rnd until you have completed K2tog rnd—6 sts rem. Break yarn, thread through tapestry needle, and draw through rem sts.

Finishing

Block stocking. Fold hem into place and stitch down with yarn.

Hanging Cord

To make braid for hanging stocking, cut three 18" lengths of each color. Holding three strands of each color tog as one, braid strands tog. Tie knots at either end of braid to secure. Sew both ends of braid to inside of stocking to make a loop.

Checkerboard chart

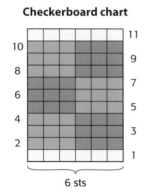

6 sts

Stripe chart

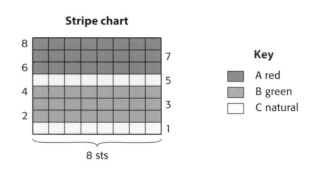

8 sts

Key

■ A red
■ B green
□ C natural

Figure chart

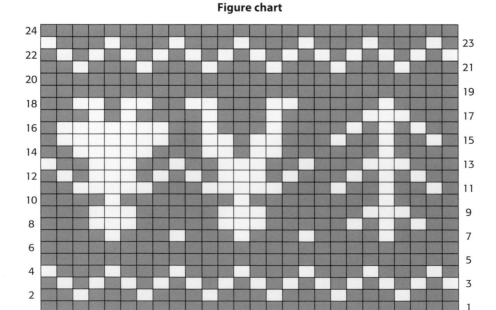

26 sts

Stripy Socks

*Nothing feels quite like hand-knit socks—
always a luxurious gift!*

Finished Sizes

To fit: 1 yr (2–4 yrs, 4–8 yrs, Adult Small, Adult
Medium, Adult Large, Adult Extra Large)
Foot circumference: 5 (5¾, 6½, 7½, 8, 8½, 9½)"
Foot length: 5 (6, 7, 8, 9, 10, 11)"

Materials

Yarn: 100% Merino wool DK-weight yarn (**3**) in the
following amounts:
   A: 120 (120, 120, 120, 120, 240, 240) yds
   B: 120 yds (all sizes)
   C: 120 yds (all sizes)
Needles: Size 4 double-pointed needles (dpns), size 6
   dpns or size required to obtain gauge
Notions: Stitch markers, stitch holder, tapestry needle

Gauge

22 sts and 30 rows = 4" in St st on size 6 needles

Rib Pattern

Rnd 1: With A, *K1, P1, rep from * around.
Rnd 2: Knit with B.
Rnd 3: With B, *K1, P1, rep from * around.
Rnd 4: Knit with C.
Rnd 5: With C, *K1, P1, rep from * around.
Rnd 6: Knit with A.

Socks

With size 4 dpns and A, CO 28 (32, 36, 42, 44, 48, 52) sts. Join, pm at beg of rnd. Beg Rib patt, carrying colors not in use up inside of sock (twist yarns loosely when changing colors), work Rib patt 5 (7, 8, 10, 12, 13, 15) times, ending last rep with rnd 5—leg should measure about 3 (4, 5, 6, 7, 8, 9)". Break B and C.

> ### Want a Looser Sock?
> If you're concerned that the sock will be too tight around the calf, knit the first inch with size 6 needles; then work the rest of the calf with size 4 needles.

Work Heel Flap

With A, K7 (8, 9, 10, 11, 12, 13) sts, turn work, and purl across 14 (16, 18, 20, 22, 24, 26) sts. Place rem 14 (16, 18, 22, 22, 24, 26) sts on holder. Change to size 6 dpn and work heel flap as follows:

Row 1: *Sl 1 pw wyib, K1, rep from * across.
Row 2: Sl first st pw wyif, purl across row.
Work these 2 rows a total of 7 (8, 9, 10, 11, 12, 13) times—14 (16, 18, 20, 22, 24, 26) rows.

Turn Heel

Row 1: K9 (10, 11, 12, 13, 14, 15), K2tog, K1, turn.
Row 2: Sl 1 pw, P5, P2tog, P1.
Row 3: Sl 1 pw, K6, K2tog, K1.
Row 4: Sl 1 pw, P7, P2tog, P1.
Cont in this manner, working 1 more st before dec on each successive row until all heel sts have been worked, ending with a purl row—10 (10, 12, 12, 14, 14, 16) sts.

Work Gusset

Still using A and size 6 dpns, K10 (10, 12, 12, 14, 14, 16) heel sts, PU 7 (8, 9, 10, 11, 12, 13) sts along selvage of heel flap, pm (this will be a gusset marker), K14 (16, 18, 22, 22, 24, 26) sts from holder, pm (another gusset marker), PU 7 (8, 9, 10, 11, 12, 13) sts along other heel-flap selvage—38 (42, 48, 54, 58, 62, 68) sts. K5 (5, 6, 6, 7, 7, 8) heel sts and replace your "beg of rnd" marker if you removed it while working the heel flap. This is now beg of rnd.

Cont stripe sequence in St st while shaping gusset. If you're unsure how to proceed, just cont stripes as est on leg.

The striped set of coordinating socks, mittens (page 15), and hat (page 5) makes a memorable gift for a new baby, a birthday, or any other special occasion.

Next rnd: Knit to 2 sts before first gusset marker, K2tog, knit to next gusset marker, SSK, knit to end of rnd.

Next rnd: Knit.

Work these 2 rnds a total of 5 (5, 6, 6, 7, 7, 8) times— 28 (32, 36, 42, 44, 48, 52) sts.

Knit Foot

Work even in St st, maintaining stripe sequence throughout until foot meas approx 4 (5, 5½, 6½, 7½, 8, 9)" from back of heel, ending with a completed stripe in color B. Break A and B. Knit 1 rnd with C.

Shape Toe

Work in C throughout.

Next rnd: K4 (5, 6, 7, 8, 9, 10), K2tog, K2, SSK, K8 (10, 12, 15, 16, 18, 20), K2tog, K2, SSK, K4 (5, 6, 8, 8, 9, 10).

Next rnd: Knit.

Next rnd: K3 (4, 5, 6, 7, 8, 9), K2tog, K2, SSK, K6 (8, 10, 13, 14, 16, 18), K2tog, K2, SSK, K3 (4, 5, 7, 7, 8, 9).

Next rnd: Knit.

Size 1 yr: Rep last 4 rnds once more, working dec as established—12 sts. Break yarn, leaving 12" tail. Divide sts over 2 needles: knit first 3 sts of next rnd, place next 6 sts on another needle, place last 3 sts on first needle—6 sts per needle. Graft the toe sts tog.

All other sizes: Rep last 4 rnds, working dec as est until (12, 16, 26, 28, 24, 32) sts rem. From this point forward, omit plain knit rnds between dec rnds. Cont dec every rnd until (12, 12, 14, 12, 12, 12) sts rem. Break yarn, leaving 12" tail. Divide sts over 2 needles: knit first 3 sts of the next rnd, place next (6, 6, 7, 6, 6, 6) sts on another needle, place last (3, 3, 4, 3, 3, 3) sts on first needle—(6, 6, 7, 6, 6, 6) sts per needle. Graft the toe sts tog.

Stripy Mittens

*When knitting mittens for gifts, consider knitting three
mittens instead of the usual two, as a hedge against the
likelihood of a misplaced mitten.*

Sizes

To fit: 1 yr (2–5 yrs, Child/Adult Small, Adult Medium,
Adult Large)
Hand circumference: 4½ (5½, 6¾, 7¾, 9)"

Materials

Yarn: Approx 110 yds *each* of 3 colors per pair of 100%
   wool DK-weight yarn (3); label colors A, B, and C
Needles: Size 4 double pointed needles (dpns), size 6
   dpns or size required to obtain gauge
Notions: Stitch markers, waste yarn, tapestry needle

Gauge

22 sts and 30 rows = 4" in St st on size 6 needles

Rib Pattern

Rnd 1: With A, *K1, P1, rep from * around.
Rnd 2: Knit with B.
Rnd 3: With B, *K1, P1, rep from * around.
Rnd 4: Knit with C.
Rnd 5: With C, *K1, P1, rep from * around.
Rnd 6: Knit with A.
Rep these 6 rnds.

Mittens

With size 4 dpns and A, CO 24 (30, 36, 42, 48) sts.
Join, pm at beg of rnd.

Make Cuff

Beg Rib patt, carrying colors not in use up inside of mitten. (Twist yarns loosely when changing colors.) Work rnds 1–6 a total of 2 (2, 3, 4, 4) times; work rnds 1–3 once more.

Knit Hand

Maintain stripe sequence throughout.

Change to size 6 dpn and St st, cont color sequence as established. Knit 3 rnds, increasing 1 st on second rnd—25 (31, 37, 43, 49) sts.

Shape Thumb Gusset

Maintain stripe sequence throughout.

Next rnd: K11 (14, 17, 20, 23), pm, (K1f&b) 2 times, pm, K12 (15, 18, 21, 24).

Next rnd: Knit.

Next rnd: K1f&b into st after first gusset marker and st before second gusset marker.

Next rnd: Knit.

Rep last 2 rnds until you have 10 (12, 14, 16, 18) sts between markers—33 (41, 49, 57, 65) sts.

Next rnd: K11 (14, 17, 20, 23), remove marker, K1, place next 9 (11, 13, 15, 17) sts on waste yarn, remove marker, inc 1 st by making a backward loop over needle, knit to end of rnd—25 (31, 37, 43, 49) sts. Work even until mitten measures 2½ (3, 4, 5, 6)" from top of ribbing, K2 (2, 2, 0, 2) tog at end of last rnd. For size Adult Medium, inc 1 st at end of last rnd. You should end with a completed stripe and 24 (30, 36, 44, 48) sts.

Shape Top

Cont stripe sequence as est, work 1 rnd even.

Next rnd: *K4 (4, 7, 9, 10), K2tog, rep from * around.

Next rnd: Knit.

Rep last 2 rnds, working 1 less st before dec with each dec rnd until you have completed K2 (2, 3, 3, 3), K2tog rnd. From this point forward, cont in color used for previous rnd and work dec rnds only until 8 (10, 8, 8, 8) sts rem. Break yarn, thread through tapestry needle, and draw through rem sts.

Work Thumb

Place thumb sts on waste yarn back onto dpn. Working in the rnd with next color in stripe sequence, PU 1 st between inside of thumb and body of mitten—10 (12, 14, 16, 18) sts. Work even in same color until solid-color portion of thumb measures 1", K2 (0, 0, 2, 0) tog on last rnd. For size Child/Adult Small, inc 1 st on last rnd—9 (12, 15, 15, 18) sts.

Next rnd: *K1 (2, 3, 3, 4), K2tog, rep from * around.

Next rnd: Knit.

Rep last 2 rnds, working 1 less st before dec with each dec rnd until 6 sts rem. Break yarn, thread through tapestry needle, and draw through rem sts.

Easy Striped Scarf

The right and wrong sides of this scarf are different, but both are colorful and appealing, giving two different wearing options.

Sizes
To fit: Child (Adult)
Measurements: 4" x 45 (55)"

Materials
Yarn: Approx 55 yds *each* of 4 colors of 100% Merino wool bulky-weight yarn (🇧); label yarns A, B, C, and D
Needles: Size 10½ circular needle (24" or longer) or size required to obtain gauge
Notions: Tapestry needle

Gauge
15 sts and 24 rows = 4" in Rib patt on size 10½ needle

Rib Pattern
Row 1: Knit with A.
Row 2: With A, *K1, P1, rep from *, end K1.
Row 3: Knit with B.
Row 4: With B, *K1, P1, rep from *, end K1.
Row 5: Knit with C.
Row 6: With C, *K1, P1, rep from *, end K1.
Row 7: Knit with D.
Row 8: With D, *K1, P1, rep from *, end K1.

Changing Colors
To carry colors neatly, always pick up the new color from below and behind the other colors. Done correctly, this makes an attractive spiral of color along the edge where the colors are carried.

Scarf
With A, CO 169 (205) sts. Starting with row 2 (CO counts as row 1), work Rib patt 3 times, BO in patt on row 8 of 3rd rep.

Keeping Edges Even
When knitting scarf horizontally, it's important to have relaxed, even tension in your cast on and bind off. If one edge is considerably tighter than the other, the scarf will torque. You don't have to use any special techniques; just take care to work in similar tension when you start and finish the scarf.

Scarf Donations
If you're interested in making a hat or scarf for the homeless, an online search can find groups that collect handmade items to distribute. Such projects are a fabulous way to use your own knitting talents to help others—just make sure to use easy-care yarns.

Embossed Heart Scarf

You can knit this snuggly bulky-weight scarf in an evening. The shorter size fits both children and adults, while the 70" version makes a dramatic scarf for grown-ups.

Sizes

To fit: Child/Adult Short (Adult Long)
Measurements: 5¾" x 43 (70)"

Materials

Yarn: 50% cotton, 50% acrylic blend bulky-weight yarn (5) in the following amounts:

Child/Adult Short: 55 yds *each* of 3 colors; label colors A, B, and C

Adult Long: 110 yds *each* of 3 colors; label colors A, B, and C

Needles: Size 10 needles or size required to obtain gauge

Notions: Tapestry needle

Gauge

13 sts and 19 rows = 4" in St st on size 10 needles

Scarf

With A, CO 19 sts. Knit 3 rows.
Beg chart: K2, work Small Heart chart, K2. Cont in patt, work through chart 3 (5) times. Change to B and work through chart 3 (5) times. Change to C and work through chart 3 (5) times. Knit 4 rows, then BO.

Finishing

Work in ends and block scarf to measurements.

Keeping It Flat

This scarf has a tendency to fold in along the garter-stitch borders. To alleviate this tendency, wash the scarf as directed on the yarn label, and then dry flat. Store the scarf rolled up from the short end when it's not being worn.

Small Heart chart

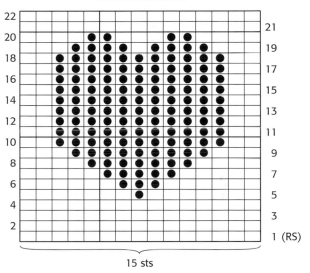

15 sts

Key

☐ Knit on RS/Purl on WS
⬤ Purl on RS/Knit on WS

A playful variation on this scarf is to use a different color for every chart repeat. Make the scarf as long or as short as you like, with as many colors as you wish.

Booties

These booties can be knit in an evening. For a really fabulous gift, knit several pairs and give them as a set.

Size
To fit: 0–6 mos
Foot circumference: 3½"
Foot length: 2¾"

Materials
Yarn: 100% cotton DK-weight yarn ③ in following amounts:
  A: Small amount
  B: 108 yds
Needles: Size 3 double-pointed needles (dpns) or size required to obtain gauge
Notions: Stitch markers, stitch holder, tapestry needle

Gauge
24 sts and 32 rows = 4" in St st on size 3 needles

Need a Different Size?
To make the booties larger or smaller, follow the pattern as written, adjusting the needle size up or down.

Booties
With A, CO 22 sts.
Starting with a purl row, work 4 rows in St st. Divide sts over 4 dpns, join, pm at beg of rnd. Knit 2 rnds. Break A. Replace marker for start of rnd between sts 6 and 7. Join B and knit 1 rnd.

Beg Heel
K10, turn work, P10. Place rem 12 sts on holder. Knit 10 rows, ending with completed WS row.

Turn Heel
Row 1: K5, K2tog, K1, turn.
Row 2: K2, K2tog, K1, turn.
Row 3: K3, K2tog, K1, turn.
Row 4: K4, K2tog, K1, turn—6 sts.
Break yarn.

Make Gusset
Sl first 3 heel sts onto another dpn, place marker (this is now beg of rnd) and rejoin B. K3, PU 5 sts along selvage of heel flap, pm (this will be a gusset marker), work 12 sts from holder as K2, SSK, K4, K2tog, K2, pm (another gusset marker), PU 5 sts along other heel-flap selvage, knit last 3 heel sts—26 sts.
Next rnd: Purl to 2 sts before first gusset marker, P2tog, knit to next gusset marker, P2tog, purl to end of rnd.
Next rnd: Knit.
Work these 2 rnds a total of 3 times—20 sts.

Work Foot
Rnd 1: P5, K10, P5.
Rnd 2: Knit.
Work rnds 1 and 2 a total of 5 times—10 rnds.
Booties should measure about 2½" from back of heel.

Shape Toe
Next rnd: P3, P2tog, SSK, K6, K2tog, P2tog, P3.
Next rnd: Knit.
Next rnd: P2, P2tog, SSK, K4, K2tog, P2tog, P2—12 sts.
Break yarn, thread through tapestry needle, and draw through rem sts.

Preemie Booties

Premature babies need booties to keep those tiny toes warm and comfy. A great way to use up your fine-gauge stash yarn is to knit several pairs of booties and donate them to your local hospital.

Embossed Heart Blanket

Sweet and simple, this is one of the quickest baby blankets you can make. The optional lining makes the blanket that much more special.

Size
30½" x 31½"

Materials
Yarn: 165 yds *each* of 3 colors of cotton-acrylic blend bulky-weight yarn **⑤**; label colors A, B, and C
Needles: Size 10 circular needle (24" long) or size required to obtain gauge
Notions: Tapestry needle
Optional: 1 yd of preshrunk cotton flannel (at least 36" wide), sewing needle, sewing thread

Gauge
13 sts and 20 rows = 4" in St st on size 10 needle

Blanket
With A, CO 99 sts. Knit 3 rows.
Beg chart: K3, work Large Heart chart 3 times, K3. Cont in patt until you have completed the chart. Change to B, work chart in same manner. Change to C, work chart in same manner. Knit 4 rows, then BO.

Tension Problems?
If you find that you have difficulty maintaining even tension as you work the blanket (not uncommon when working with a bulky cotton yarn), don't despair. After finishing the blanket, just wash and dry it according to the label specifications and you'll find that the tension evens itself out beautifully.

Finishing
Work in ends and block blanket to measurements.
Optional lining: Preshrink flannel, cut fabric to 30½" x 31½", serge edges or fold under ½" all the way around, pin fabric to WS of blanket and hand stitch in place with sewing needle and thread.

Large Heart chart

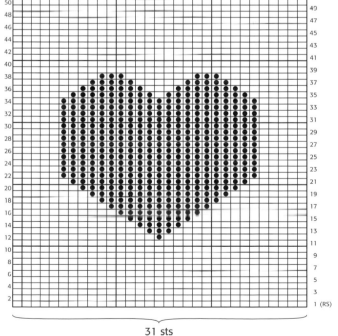

31 sts

Key

☐	Knit on RS/Purl on WS
⊡	Purl on RS/Knit on WS

Patchwork Blanket

Garter stitch worked in strips makes this blanket an ideal group or charitable giving project.

Size

37" x 39"

Materials

Yarn: 100% Superwash wool Aran-weight yarn ④ in the following amounts:

A: 195 yds (gold)

B: 260 yds (red)

C: 325 yds (purple)

D: 325 yds (blue)

E: 325 yds (green)

Needles: Size 9 needles or size required to obtain gauge

Notions: Tapestry needle, 1¼ yds of preshrunk cotton flannel (at least 36" wide), sewing needle, sewing thread

Gauge

16 sts and 30 rows = 4" in garter stitch on size 9 needles

Blanket

Worked in garter stitch: knit every row. Cast ons and bind offs are not included in row count.

For each strip, CO 22 sts using color indicated on chart. Work each color block for 40 rows (you'll have 20 garter-stitch ridges per square); then change colors as indicated on chart. Make 7 strips as shown in chart.

Finishing

Sew strips together as shown in chart. It will be easier to sew the strips together if you assemble them all with the cast-on edge at the bottom and the bound-off edge at the top. That way, the two edges to be seamed appear absolutely identical as you work. Don't worry about changing the color of the seaming yarn with every color change in the strip; just pick whatever color is used most in the strips you're seaming.

Borders

With E, PU 148 sts along selvage, knit 6 rows, then BO. Rep along other selvage.

With E, PU 148 sts along lower edge, knit 6 rows, then BO. Rep along upper edge.

Optional Lining

Preshrink flannel, cut fabric to 37" x 39", serge edges or fold under ½" all the way around, pin fabric to WS of blanket and hand stitch in place with sewing needle and thread.

Want a Different Size?

Make the blanket bigger or smaller simply by adjusting the yarn and needle size. Chunkier yarn and bigger needles will result in a bigger blanket; finer yarn and smaller needles make a smaller blanket. Just remember that if you're doing the Patchwork Blanket as a group project, everyone needs to knit at the same gauge.

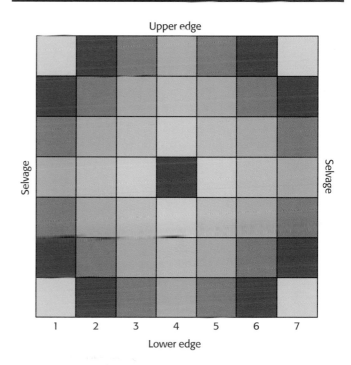

Each strip is worked vertically in garter stitch—7 strips total. Each square is 22 sts wide by 40 rows tall; you will have 20 garter-stitch "ridges" per square. Cast-on and bind-off rows not included in row count.

Appliquéd Purse and Scarf

These quick-and-easy projects make wonderful gifts for the little girls in your life. Omit the flower appliqué, and the scarf works well for little boys, too.

Sizes

Purse: 5½" x 5½"

Scarf: 4" x 43½"

Materials

Yarn: Approx 190 yds of 80% pima cotton, 20% wool blend worsted-weight yarn (4) in 4 different colors. (The yarn quantities listed are enough to make two purses and two scarves, provided that each is made in a different color.)

Needles: Size 6 needles or size required to obtain gauge; size 5 double-pointed needles (dpns) for purse, flowers, and leaves

Notions: Snap for each purse closure, tapestry needle

Gauge

23 sts and 28 rows = 4" in Chessboard patt for scarf or purse on size 6 needles

Chessboard Pattern for Scarf

Rows 1, 3, and 5 (RS): *K7, P5, rep from *, end K1.

Row 2: P1, *K5, P7, rep from * across.

Rows 4, 6, 8, and 10: Knit the knit sts, purl the purl sts.

Rows 7, 9, and 11: K1 *P5, K7, rep from * across.

Row 12: Knit the knit sts, purl the purl sts.

Rep rows 1–12 rows for patt.

Chessboard Pattern for Purse

Rows 1, 3, and 5 (RS): K7, *P5, K7, rep from * across.

Row 2: P7, *K5, P7, rep from * across.

Rows 4, 6, 8, and 10: Knit the knit sts, purl the purl sts.

Rows 7, 9, and 11: K1, *P5, K7, rep from *, end P5, K1.

Row 12: Knit the knit sts, purl the purl sts.

Rep rows 1–12 rows for patt.

Scarf

With size 6 needles, CO 25 sts. Starting with row 2, work in Chessboard patt for Scarf until scarf meas 43½" (50 patt blocks worked), ending with completed row 5 of patt. BO in patt on next row. Weave in ends and block scarf to measurements. Make flowers and leaves as directed on page 30 and sew on to lower edge of scarf.

Purse

With size 6 needles, CO 31 sts. Starting with row 2, work in Chessboard patt for Purse until purse meas 10", ending with completed row 12 of patt (12 patt blocks worked).

Shape flap: On RS rows, dec 1 st at each side EOR 9 times—13 sts rem. BO in patt.

Weave in ends and block purse. Fold lower edge of purse up to meet base of flap. Whipstitch side seams tog.

I-cord strap: With size 5 dpns, CO 3 sts. Work I-cord as follows: K3, *do not turn. Slide sts to opposite end of needle and K3, rep from * until strip is 32" or desired length. BO. Position each end of strap at least 2" down inside purse and sew along entire 2" on each end. Make flowers and leaves as directed below and sew onto flap. Sew snap in place.

Flowers and Leaves

For each purse or scarf, make 1 full flower, 1 half flower, and 1 leaf using a different color for each piece.

Full Flower

With size 5 dpns, CO 49 sts.

Row 1: P6, *K1, P5, rep from * to last 7 sts, end K1, P6.

Row 2: K2, *sl 2 tog kw, K1, p2sso, K1, P1, K1, rep from * to last 5 sts, end S2KP, K2.

Row 3: Knit the knit sts and purl the purl sts.

Row 4: K1, *sl 2 tog kw, K1, p2sso, P1, rep from * to last 4 sts, end S2KP, K1.

Row 5: Knit the knit sts and purl the purl sts.

Break yarn, leaving 6" tail. With tapestry needle, thread yarn through loops on knitting needle and gather knitting into circle. Seam edges. Work in ends.

Half Flower

With size 5 dpns, CO 25 sts.

Rep rows 1–5 of Full Flower.

Break yarn, leaving 6" tail. With tapestry needle, thread yarn through loops on knitting needle and gather knitting into half circle. Work in ends.

Leaf

With size 5 dpns, CO 13 sts.

Row 1: P6, K1, P6.

Rep rows 2–5 of Full Flower.

Break yarn, leaving 6" tail. With tapestry needle, thread yarn through loops on knitting needle and gather knitting into wedge. Work in ends.

Sew together as follows: Sew the half flower underneath the full flower so it just peeks out from the full flower. Sew the leaf to the flowers in the same fashion. Sew the completed flower to the scarf or purse flap about ¾ of the way out from the center, not at the edges. Make a French knot in the center of the full flower using the leaf-color yarn. Note: It's easier to make the French knot after sewing the completed flower to the purse ⅔ of the way around. After making the French knot, sew the rest of the flower.

Knitting Abbreviations

[ ]	Work instructions within brackets as many times as directed.
( )	Work instructions within parentheses in the place directed.
*	Repeat instructions following the single asterisk as directed.
"	inch(es)
approx	approximately
beg	begin(ning)
BO	bind off
CC	contrasting color
CO	cast on
cont	continue
dec	decrease(ing)
dpn(s)	double-pointed needle(s)
EOR	every other row
est	established
foll	follow(ing)
inc(s)	increase(ing)(s)
K	knit
K1f&b	knit into front and back of same stitch—1 stitch increased
K2tog	knit 2 stitches together
K3tog	knit 3 stitches together
kw	knitwise
LH	left hand
M1	make 1 stitch
MC	main color
meas	measure(s)
mm	millimeter(s)
P	purl
patt	pattern
P2tog	purl 2 stitches together
pm	place marker
prev	previous
psso	pass slipped stitch over
p2sso	pass 2 slipped stitches over
PU	pick up and knit
pw	purlwise
rem	remaining
rep	repeat
RH	right hand
rnd(s)	round(s)
RS	right side(s)
sc	single crochet
SKP	slip 1, knit 1, pass stitch over the knit stitch—1 stitch decreased
S2KP	slip 2 stitches knitwise, knit 1, pass 2 slipped stitches over the knit stitch—2 stitches decreased
sl	slip
sl st	slip stitch
ssk	slip, slip, knit these 2 stitches together—a decrease
st(s)	stitch(es)
St st	stockinette stitch
tbl	through back loop
tog	together
WS	wrong side(s)
wyib	with yarn in back
wyif	with yarn in front
yd(s)	yard(s)
YO	yarn over

Helpful Information

Metric Conversion Chart

m	=	yds	x	0.9144
yds	=	m	x	1.0936
g	=	oz	x	28.35
oz	=	g	x	0.0352

Standard Yarn-Weight System

Yarn-Weight Symbol and Category Name	**0** Lace	**1** Super Fine	**2** Fine	**3** Light	**4** Medium	**5** Bulky	**6** Super Bulky
Types of Yarn in Category	Fingering, 10-count crochet thread	Sock, Fingering, Baby	Sport, Baby	DK, Light Worsted	Worsted, Afghan, Aran	Chunky, Craft, Rug	Bulky, Roving
Knit Gauge Range* in Stockinette Stitch to 4"	33 to 40 sts	27 to 32 sts	23 to 26 sts	21 to 24 sts	16 to 20 sts	12 to 15 sts	6 to 11 sts
Recommended Needle in Metric Size Range	1.5 to 2.25 mm	2.25 to 3.25 mm	3.25 to 3.75 mm	3.75 to 4.5 mm	4.5 to 5.5 mm	5.5 to 8 mm	8 mm and larger
Recommended Needle in US Size Range	000 to 1	1 to 3	3 to 5	5 to 7	7 to 9	9 to 11	11 and larger

These are guidelines only. The above reflect the most commonly used gauges and needle sizes for specific yarn categories.